ABSTRACT HEART

J. IRON WORD

To my love

without you there

are no words.

CHAPTERS

TRUTHS
(7)

HER
(63)

L O V E
(1 1 9)

H U R T
(1 9 1)

L A S T C H A P T E R
(2 1 5)

TRUTHS

BLINK

It seems that those
with the biggest
hearts are the first
to go; almost as if
they know and they
love enough for a
lifetime in less than
a blink.

1-17-15 / j. iron word

MOST BEAUTIFUL

The most beautiful
humans are the
ones with the
heaviest hearts;
loving the hardest
while hurting the
deepest.

12-4-14 / j. iron word

FEROCITY

The only thing
we ever really
want is to be
loved by
someone, with the same
ferocity in which we love.

5-16-15 / j. iron word

All Or Nothing

I am not a casual kind of
lover; I am an all or
nothing kind of soul.

12-24-15 / j. iron word

BEAUTIFUL MESS

We are all a
mess, but it is how we
keep it together that makes us
beautiful.

8-13-15 / j. iron word

Kid At Heart

The greatest adults are still kids at
heart. They have not forgotten it
is the small things that mean the
most.

5-15-15 / j. iron word

FLY

"What do you plan to do
with those wings, everyone
knows humans can't fly?" "I'm
not everyone, I am me and I am a
dreamer and a doer."

3-2-16 / j. iron word

FLAWLESS IMPERFECTIONS

We are all bits and pieces of
flawless imperfections.

11-27-14 / j. iron word

SHINE

Dirty chandeliers still shine and broken hearts still beat.

3-20-15 / j. iron word

MORE COMPLETE

There is something about being broken, at various times in your life; that makes you a more complete person.

1-16-15 / j. iron word

THE STRONGEST

Even the strongest hands lose
their grip and the biggest hearts
still break.

4-13-15 / j. iron word

CRAVE

If love were
easy, we
wouldn't
crave it.

5-16-15 / j. iron word

TOUGH LOVE

I just want to be
with someone who
doesn't disappear
when love gets
tough.

8-1-15 / j. iron word

*A*GAIN

Sometimes tears have to
fall and hearts have to
hurt.

Before you can smile and
love again.

1-12-16 / j. iron word

SURVIVORS DO

I have always been
attracted to the
broken. Not
because I want to
fix them, I don't
want to fix anyone. I can't even fix
myself. Rather, I know we
connect on another level, a real
one. We know what pain feels
like-- to sleep with a broken heart,
only to wake up to paint a smile
on your face and act as if
everything is "okay." Because
that's what people like me do, like
we do, like survivors do.

7-17-15 / j. iron word

WHATEVER IT TAKES

Relationships
are not always
50/50; they are
about both
partners doing whatever it takes,
whenever needed.

9-29-15 / j. iron word

LOYALTY

We are not looking for a
sometimes kind of love. What
we need is the kind of love that
never leaves.

10-28-15 / j. iron word

LOVE SENSE

I tried to love logically,
but it didn't make sense.

3-1-15 / j. iron word

Magic Love

All we ever ask for is a little magic
and a whole lot of love, but to us
they are one in the same.

11-30-15 / j. iron word

THE LOUDEST CRAVING

I live loud, but only
prefer to be myself
with a select few. I
do not seek the
attention of many,
but crave it from
just one.

5-20-15 / j. iron word

FOREVER IMPERFECTION

I am done with
incomplete loves and
almost forevers; just give
me an old fashioned
imperfection that lasts as
long as I do.

11-30-15 / j. iron word

LISTEN

Always make an effort to listen, especially when they do not say a word.

10-13-15 / j. iron word

TOMORROW CONVERSATIONS

There's something
special about losing
track of time in a
conversation that leads
you into tomorrow.

10-27-16 / j. iron word

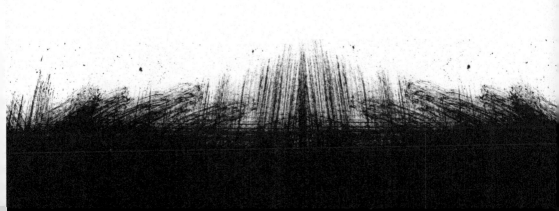

TEMPORARY

We never really
belong to anyone,
but ourselves and even that is
temporary.

11-30-15 / j. iron word

MEMORY LANE

I took a walk down
memory lane today, for
the first time in years. It
was longer than I
remembered, but every bit as
beautiful as when you were
still here.

5-3-15 / j. iron word

MIDDLE

From the beginning I knew we
would have an end, but more than
anything I wanted to see how we
would love in the middle.

12-9-15 / j. iron word

LESSON IN LIVING

Always teach them there is
nothing they cannot be, even if it
is the moon.

12-15-15 / j. iron word

SETTLE FOR EVERYTHING

Never settle for
someone's second
anything, when you are worthy
of being someone's everything.

12-16-15 / j. iron word

*F*AIRY *T*ALE *L*OVE

I have loved long enough to
know it does not always end
in happily ever after. I have
also lived long enough to
know, happily ever after is not
just for fairy tales.

6-21-16 / j. iron word

SAND

I write secrets in the
sand, knowing the
tide will never
whisper them.

2-16-15 / j. iron word

UNIQUE

I am not any
person you have
ever been with, therefore do not
treat me like every human that
you have been.

5-20-16 / j. iron word

DIFFERENT

Maybe I am
different, but I
do not see
people in my life as part of a
game. If I am your friend I am
loyal until my last breath and if I
love you it's until my last beat.

5-20-16 / j. iron word

BY ONE

I am not one to
share or be
shared; I love one
and am loved by
one.

4-29-15 / j. iron word

BELIEVE

And when they
ask me what it is I
believe in, I will
simply reply,
"love."

3-12-16 / j. iron word

41

Soul Fire

Sexy does not come from
the shape of a body, but the
fire in a soul.

5-28-15 / j. iron word

RE-FOCUS

People like to focus on what they
cannot do, but they fail to see the
world they can create with what
they can.

3-12-16 / j. iron word

SOUL RECOGNITION

It's funny how
complete
strangers can
have familiar
souls.

4-25-16 / j. iron word

BREATHE

Be you, the real you,
because all of you is
beautiful; even
your bad needs to
breathe.

10-28-15 / j. iron word

NOTHING BEHIND

I am not the type of
person to come back for
anything, because I never
leave what I love behind.

6-13-15 / j. iron word

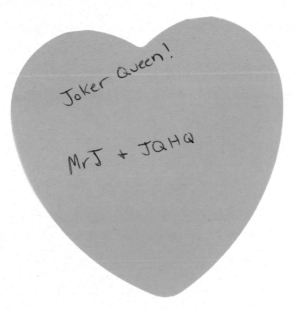

Joker Queen!

MrJ + JQHQ

ONE QUEEN

Treat her like a princess, but
make sure she knows she is your
one and only queen.

10-25-15 / j. iron word

UNFORGETTABLE

I don't know where you're
going, but I hope I am a
stop in your life. Even if you
stay for a minute, I promise
you'll remember me for a
lifetime.

1-5-15 / j. iron word

CONVICTION

We do not want to be loved with
confliction.
We want to be loved with
conviction.

5-14-15 / j. iron word

HANG ON

Maybe we hang on so tightly,
because we worry of letting go of
a once in a lifetime kind of love,
too soon.

3-14-16 / j. iron word

HEART LESSONS

"Hey heart when will you
learn?"
"That's not my job brain."

9-4-15 / j. iron word

MENDED

Sometimes things have to
become completely undone
before they can be mended.

9-24-15 / j. iron word

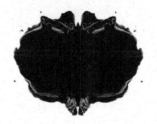

FIRST SECOND

You can know someone
your entire life and they
may never really know you.
Yet there are those
you meet and from
the first second you feel as if
you've known them forever and a
day.

8-28-15 / j. iron word

NAKED TRUTH

If you tell
someone
everything
there is to know
about you and
they love you
more
for it, never let
them go.

8-17-15 / j. iron word

REMEMBER

Smile hard
and laugh
harder, because
love is always
possible.

5-24-15 / j. iron word

SPARK

Do not be the one
to sit back and let
life happen, be the
spark that sets it on
fire.

6-10-15 / j. iron word

THE END

We meet many matches in
our lives, but there is
always one that burns
brighter and hotter than the
rest. Our only hope is that they
will be the one burning beside us
in the end.

12-8-15 / j. iron word

CURVED

Perfect is for
straight lines
and edges, I'm
as curved as my heart.

11-30-15 / j. iron word

FOREVER EFFORT

Put effort in everything you
do and when you do find someone
who loves as hard as you do it will
never fail or fade.

10 31 16 / j. iron word

STRENGTH

I have stumbled more
than a time or two and I have
the scars to prove it, but I also
have the strength from picking
myself back up again.

11-6-16 / j. iron word

THE JOURNEY

Sometimes you have to walk
a long way in the wrong direction,
to get to where you are going.

1-13-15 / j. iron word

LOVE WORTH

Be with someone who fights for you,
someone who knows you are worth it,
someone who knows love is worth it.

10-23-15 / j. iron word

OLD SOUL

She is a throwback to a time when
love didn't cost a thing, but was
everything.

10-3-15 / j. iron word

64

GYPSY

She is a gypsy with a winged soul
whom the stars cannot contain; a
wanderer of the universe, whose
paradise is never lost, but always
found beneath
her feet.

4-14-15 / j. iron word

WORTH THE FIGHT

She does not approve of violence,
but she wants someone to show
her she is worth
fighting for.

5-7-15 / j. iron word

SHE'S EVERYTHING

She's not your typical
anything, but somehow
uniquely everything.

10-9-16 / j. iron word

THORNS

She didn't want to be
loved for her petals,
she wanted to be loved
for her thorns. She
knew if someone loved
her flaws, they would
love her whole.

8-24-16 / j. iron word

*W*ILD

Her messy hair is a visible
attribute of her stubborn spirit. As
she shakes it free, she
smiles knowing wild is
her favorite color.

5-16-15 / j. iron word

CRAZY BEAUTIFUL

The most beautiful minds have a
hint of crazy and she is no
different.

6-17-15 / j. iron word

HOPE

She reminds me that
beauty isn't skin deep,
that love is infinite and hope is a
place that lives inside of us.

3-6-16 / j. iron word

ALL SEASONS

She is the kind of girl who walks
with you in the pouring rain, runs
with you under the light of the
moon and blossoms
under the rays of the
sun.

1-20-16 / j. iron word

SHE IS HER

She is not the girl you dreamt her
to be; she's the woman she
dreamed of being.

3-10-16 / j. iron word

GREATEST LOVE

"I forgot to tell you that I love you," she said to herself and smiled.

3-19-16 / j. iron word

SELF-ASSEMBLED

She picked up the
pieces of her own
broken heart and
reassembled it
herself.
She doesn't need to be saved, just
loved.

5-13-15 / j. iron word

NATURALLY

She didn't try to be sexy;
it just came naturally, but
when she did she sent the
world up in flames.

1-4-15 / j. iron word

THE BEST

She is easy to fall for
and hard to get over. She's the
best any soul could ever love.

4-24-15 / j. iron word

GOOD AND CRAZY

She is damn good at being bad,
but you have to love her good and
crazy, before she shows you what
that means.

12-3-15 / j. iron word

THE LOOK

She has a look of
innocence that tells you she is full
of the best kind of bad.

6-20-16 / j. iron word

HER TRUTH

She is a one
of a kind
beauty, but
there is a
truth behind
the sadness
in her eyes; a
reality that few will ever know or
understand.

9-5-14 / j. iron word

BEAUTIFUL SAVAGE

She may be a beauty, but she can
be all savage.

5-25-16 / j. iron word

SHE'S A WONDER

She's no Barbie.
She is Wonder Woman,
with a sailor's mouth.

4-11-15 / j. iron word

INDEPENDENT HEART

She's a grown woman
with an independent
heart, but that doesn't
mean she doesn't want
to be loved in between
her heartbeats.

11-2-16 / j. iron word

Iron Wings

Her beauty is the
first thing you may
notice, but delicate
she isn't; she's a
butterfly with iron wings.

8-3-15 / j. iron word

84

FIRE

While she is
comfortable in
sweat, that does
not mean she is
not perfection in
a dress; she is fire
in anything.

7-17-15 / j. iron word

UNFILTERED

Rose-colored reflections are
only a part of her whole.
A closer look reveals an
unfiltered soul that cries of a
silent fire devouring her from
the inside out.
Are you to be a witness to her
imprisonment or an outlet for
her flames?

5-18-16 / j. iron word

ORGANIZED CHAOS

She is pure in heart
and organized chaos in
soul. Love is her native
tongue, but it is not
spoken from her lips it
screams from within.
She is a beacon of hope,
in a cascading world of
despair.

5-12-15 / j. iron word

STRONG

She is the kind of strong that
makes you feel weak in the knees,
heart and mind.

5-24-16 / j. iron word

COMPLETE MISS

People who
judged her by her
looks alone,
missed her
completely.

1-26-15 / j. iron word

VISIONARY

She likes to think people are good
and some may say she is naive for
it, but maybe just maybe, she is a
visionary.

3-10-15 / j. iron word

UNFADED

She appreciates
compliments, but the last
thing she wants to be
known for is her looks. She
knows, one day her beauty will
fade and would rather be loved
for her heart and mind.

4-27-15 / j. iron word

Unraveled

She is the kind of
woman you never
stop loving, the kind
who unravels your
heart around her entire existence.

5-3-15 / j. iron word

ONE OF ONE

> She's a butterfly with
> a broken wing and
> bleeding feathers, but
> still she flies...
> but still, she flies.

7-13-15 / j. iron word

TIMELESS

She is forever young with an old soul; timeless in her beauty and class.

8-5-15 / j. iron word

TROUBLE

She has a look that tells you
you're in the best kind of
trouble; the kind you never want
to get out of.

8-27-15 / j. iron word

Up

She is different; she still looks up
even when the stars aren't
shining.

10-30-15 / j. iron word

HER MARK

She may look innocent, but
she knows how to leave
her mark.

11-11-15 / j. iron word

WILD SIDE

She didn't just walk on
the wild side she lived
there, dancing in the
streets and setting fire
to its sky.

12-8-15 / j. iron word

CRAZY ADDICTION

She is far from sane, but she is the
right kind of crazy, the kind you
get addicted to.

8-19-15 / j. iron word

WRONG LOVE

There was nothing
wrong with how she
loved, but there was,
in the way she had
been loved.

11-8-14 / j. iron word

TALENT

She has a talent
for falling down,
but even more
for getting back
up again.

12-2-15 / j. iron word

STRANGE BEAUTY

She found beauty in the strangest
places, in the broken and
forgotten. She knew the truest
hearts were the ones that
resembled hers.

12-25-15 / j. iron word

SUN

She likes to say
"I am just me,"
but what else is the
sun supposed to
say.

12-16-15 / j. iron word

SIMPLE MATH

The way I see it, 1% of
her is more than 100% of
anyone else.

4-13-15 / j. iron word

FOREVER YOUNG

She is the type of girl who will
keep you young in mind and soul;
with a heart that loves forever
and a mind that never rests.

8-9-15 / j. iron word

WHO SHE IS

People who thought she didn't
care, did not know her at all. She
was love, it just took the right soul
to see it.

2-10-16 / j. iron word

Gentleman Savage

She loves a gentleman, but she craves a savage.

8-15-15 / j. iron word

HURRICANE

You can't fall in love
with a hurricane
and expect to keep
her in a box. You fell
for her winds, let her
be the force she was
born to be.

7-25-16 / j. iron word

Sweet Heart

Her mouth is as sweet
as her heart, but her
tongue, well that's a
different story entirely.

4-22-15 / j. iron word

*B*AD

She's bad as fuck,
but in all the right
ways.

3-20-15 / j. iron word

110

PERFECT STORM

She is a perfect storm,
the kind of woman that
makes you believe love
lives in lightning bolts.

12-8-15 / j. iron word

LOVE TEARS

The water that flows
from her eyes is not pain it is love.

3-22-15 / j. iron word

CHAOTIC MASTERPIECE

She calls herself
flawed, but hers
fall into place like a masterpiece
of chaotic beauty.

12-1-15 / j. iron word

GLOW

She is perfect in any
shade; glowing when
others would fade.

11-30-15 / j. iron word

NEVER

Never be the
one to tell her
she can't, because she can and she
will, with or without you.

5-7-15 / j. iron word

SMILE

Though life
had burned
her, she wore
a smile that told the world, she
had left her sadness behind.

12-16-15 / j. iron word

STAR DUST

When she dies
someone will
throw her ashes in the sky, so she
can live with the stars where she
belongs.

2-20-16 / j. iron word

CONVERSATIONS

I talk to the moon about you with
the hope that God is listening.

1-18-16 / j. iron word

ONE

I don't want a million matches; I
want one eternal flame.

8-7-14 / j. iron word

EVERYTHING

When we were nothing more
than strangers, I loved everything
about you; I just had not met you
yet.

2-12-16 / j. iron word

PARTNER

I want a partner in
life, someone with
an opinion and
backbone. Someone
who isn't afraid to
tell me that I am
wrong and show me
how I can be better. I want
someone to tell me what they
want and even occasionally
convince me, that I want it too.

10-6-15 / j. iron word

UNFOUND LOVE

I did not find my love.
My love did not find me.
We came upon each other and
fell, together.

4-25-15 / j. iron word

CONNECTED

Maybe I
haven't known
you for
forever, but it only takes a second
to know what a forever kind of
connection feels like.

12-22-15 / j. iron word

DREAMERS

She said, "forgive me
for being a dreamer"
and he took her by the
hand and replied.
"Forgive me for not
being here sooner, to
dream with you."

5-13-15 / j. iron word

TELL ME

Tell me
your past so
I may
understand
you but give me your now, so I
may love you.

4-25-15 / j. iron word

TRUE VISION

"I wish more people
saw me in your eyes,"
she said.

And he sighed, knowing
what he saw in her
could never be seen
just with eyes.

11-5-16 / j. iron word

HOME

I want you to place your ear on
my chest and listen, to the heart
that has always beat for you, but
has yet to be heard.

4-14-16 / j. iron word

"*This*

Even if we can
never be
anything more
than this, I find
solace knowing
"this" is more
than some people
ever get.

6-6-15 / j. iron word

MY WISH

I wish I could kiss you in the
middle of the day
just because,
squeeze your
hand, look you in
the eye and say I
love you. In the
end all I ever
want is for you to
know I am there,
no matter what.

2-29-16 / j. iron word

SOMETHING ABOUT

There is something about the way
you love me, that
makes me believe
in a forever
together.

7-14-15 / j. iron word

OUR LOVE

We love in a way that others
might not understand, but it's not
about them.

2-21-15 / j. iron word

ONLY YOU

You are the only
person I see in the
most crowded rooms or
busiest of thoughts.

9-26-15 / j. iron word

PEOPLE IN LOVE

I think of you in the oddest times
and the craziest places, but I guess
that's what people in love do.

10-31-15 / j. iron word

NEVER

You are the kind
of person I hope I
never have to say goodbye to, the
type I want to have "do you
remember when?" conversations
with.

7-30-16 / j. iron word

MOON DREAMS

I am awake
when I should be sleeping, but
thoughts of you and I are playing
in my mind like a movie screen on
the moon.

8-3-15 / j. iron word

SIMPLY BEAUTIFUL

She calls herself
imperfect and simple,
but to me she is far
from simple and
entirely imperfectly beautiful.

8-31-15 / j. iron word

SHADED

If beautiful was a color your soul
would be every shade.

12-20-15 / j. iron word

139

YOUR PERSON

I want to be the person you lose
track of time with, the one you
miss after saying goodbye, the
one you countdown to see again.

5-17-15 / j. iron word

SILENT WHISPERS

Even when
we were not talking, I whispered
"good morning" and "goodnight"
to you. Hoping wherever you were
you would hear me.

3-11-15 / j. iron word

EVERYTHING

When they asked
him what makes her
beautiful, all he
could say was
"everything."

5-4-15 / j. iron word

GROW TOGETHER

If I could stop time I wouldn't,
because I want to grow old with
you.

5-12-15 / j. iron word

FUTURE MEMORIES

I caught myself
smiling
thinking of a
memory we
have yet to make; I'll let you know
when we get there.

7-6-15 / j. iron word

THE ONE

I want to be the one
you call in the middle
of the night because
you can't sleep. The
one you reach for when
you have a bad dream,
and the one you kiss
when you realize you
and I together are your
dream come true.

9-3-15 / j. iron word

LOOK

I do not need to listen to
people's lies to know
what you are not.
I only need to look into
your eyes to know
who you are.

5-22-15 / j. iron word

2

She's more than a handful, but I
have two hands; one for her
naughty and one for her nice.

7-6-15 / j. iron word

LOVE TALKS

"Hey heart, are you
awake?"

"Yeah brain I am."

"What are you doing?"

"Beating for her and you?"

"Thinking of her."

11-14-15 / j. iron word

NEVERENDING

In a
world
where
everything ends, I want to give
you a never-ending kind of love.

9-4-15 / j. iron word

HOPELESS LOVE

I am a hopeless romantic and I fall
hard and fast, but love long and
hard, for the right one.

7-4-15 / j. iron word

Moon Roots

She is the kind of girl who could
make you feel like the only man
in the world, from a thousand
miles away. The
kind that will make
you want to put
roots down, on the
moon.

9-12-15 / j. iron word

ANYWHERE

Anywhere with you, is
everywhere I want to be.

10-29-15 / j. iron word

DREAM LOVER

If I woke up tomorrow and you
were a dream, I would fall back to
sleep with
the hope
of finding
you again.

5-15-15 / j. iron word

WHAT MATTERS

Maybe not everything I wanted
was meant to be, but you and I
were and that is all that matters.

11-24-15 / j. iron word

LOOKING FORWARD

You always make tomorrows
something to look forward to and
my todays something to dream
about.

11-27-15 / j. iron word

LOVE LESSONS

Even if we could begin again I
wouldn't, because the good,
the bad and the ugly of us
has taught me the meaning
of love.

12-6-15 / j. iron word

ON HER OWN

She stands firmly on her own two
feet and I just behind
her; should she ever
need me.

2-10-15 / j. iron word

HOPEFUL DREAMER

You will always be the dreamer I
fell for, and I will always be the
one hoping to be a part of them.

12-3-15 / j. iron word

PERFECT

You are the
right kind
of wrong,
the best kind of bad and the
perfect kind of love.

12-10-15 / j. iron word

FLUENT

Passion is a language we both
speak fluently, without words.

12-15-15 / j. iron word

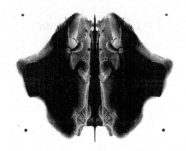

THE BURIAL

Let us unlock the
skeletons in our closets and bury
them together.

12-16-15 / j. iron word

LOVE PARTS

You found parts of me I did not
know existed, and in you, I found
a love I no longer believed was
real.

2-13-16 / j. iron word

BEAUTIFUL REFLECTION

Show me the parts of you that
you are ashamed of and I will
show you a reflection so beautiful
you will fall in love.

1-19-16 / j. iron word

HOLDING EVERYTHING

When I hold you, I
know what it feels
like to have
everything I have
ever wanted.

4-18-15 / j. iron word

ANYTHING LESS

I am sorry you
listened to a single
word of the lies
they told you, it was only a
weapon of hate and control; to
make you think you were less
than extraordinary.

5-1-16 / j. iron word

SAME ROOF

There was a moment when I
looked at you and realized that
we are closer than ever to being
one another's everyday reality; a
life when our goodnights will
happen under the same roof.

5-24-16 / j. iron word

RIGHT BESIDE

Some people take a place in our minds
and never leave our thoughts.

Some people take a place in our hearts
and keep us company even
between the beats.

Some people take a place in our lives
and remain in darkness or in light.

You are not simply some people, you
are that person and right beside you is
where I will always be.

11-13-16 / j. iron word

CALM STORM

You are my
calm, my
storm and
everything
in between.

8-17-15 / j. iron word

EVERY YESTERDAY

On the day we met, it felt as if
we knew each other for every
yesterday we had ever
known.

3-31-16 / j. iron word

SOUL CRAVINGS

I crave you whole, not simply for the skin that rests on your bones, but for the mind behind your eyes, the heart that loves inside your ribs and the fire that burns within your soul.

4-13-16 / j. iron word

LOST

I still lose myself when
I look at you, as if I am
seeing love for the first
time.

11-12-15 / j. iron word

171

WHAT IT TAKES

We take turns starting fires and burning for the other, but that is what it takes to share a lifetime of passion.

3-12-16 / j. iron word

KISS ME

Before I sleep, kiss me as if I will
never wake up, and love me in a
way I have never
known.

9-10-15 / j. iron word

I WONDER

I wonder if you can hear "I love you," in my voice when we talk.

3-23-16 / j. iron word

PERFECT MIX

You are the perfect mix of
everything I have ever craved.

4-16-16 / j. iron word

TOUCH

If I ever were to touch you, I can
only promise to break you in the
most beautiful way, beneath my
lips and fingertips.

5-31-16 / j. iron word

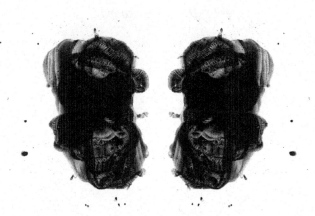

IMAGINARY LOVE

You were the greatest thing to ever happen to me, even though we only existed in my imagination.

6-11-16 / j. iron word

P.S.

PS: I am yours, it does not matter who it is, my heart only knows you.

6-21-16 / j. iron word

TWISTED

I wonder what it
feels like to wake up
next to you and
never become
anything more than
tangled; just twisted
limbs, tongues and
colliding souls.

6-23-16 / j. iron word

UNDERSTOOD

For all the sense I do not
make to others, I
somehow make
complete sense to you.

5-28-16 / j. iron word

MOON FLAME

You are an old soul and my twin
flame. Even from the dark side of
the moon, I could feel your fire.

10-14-15 / j. iron word

MORE

I wish there was more to you and
I, like we could be an us, and
every hurt we ever knew could
be buried in our before.

9-18-15 / j. iron word

STILL

Even with tears in my eyes, my heart still knows
its destiny is with you.

6-16-16 / j. iron word

MY DREAMS

There is a place between
saying goodnight and
good morning, where I always
hope we will meet.

5-22-15 / j. iron word

NAUGHTIEST BUTTERFLIES

You give me the naughtiest of
butterflies, the kind that flutter
behind my desires and explode
with your touch.

6-3-16 / j. iron word

MORE

Maybe it is in
the way my
heart feels
when I am
with you or
how your
hand settles
in mine. The
feeling of you beneath my lips or
in the way we look at one
another, but the hours we spend
together feel like nothing more
than seconds and only leave me
craving more of you, more of us.

6-12-16 / j. iron word

UNWALLED

Without walls, you are
the most beautiful
human I have ever met.

8-9-16 / j. iron word

BIASED

You like to say my
opinion is biased
and maybe it is,
but mine sees you
with an unconditional heart.

6-15-16 / j. iron word

NEVER BEEN

When I see you I'll kiss
you like you've never
been kissed, because I
miss you like you've
never been missed.

11-13-16 / j. iron word

SOULMATES

Upon being asked if soulmates existed, he removed a picture from his wallet and held it up as he said, "without a doubt."

12-24-15 / j. iron word

Go On

No matter how much you love
someone, sometimes you have to
show them, that your life can and
will go on without them.

9-14-15 / j. iron word

THREADED HEART

She was not a material girl,
but when the people that
mattered most hurt her she
shopped; with the hope that the
fabric she found would cover her
pain and the threads would keep
her heart from falling apart.

10-17-14 / j. iron word

LESS AND LESS

I have given too much of myself
to the wrong people. I want to
love and be loved, but there is that
jaded side of me that would prefer
just to stay alone. Stay within my
walls, my thoughts, my emotions
and not give my heart away
again, because every time I do I
get less of it back.

7-19-15 / j. iron word

UNREQUITED

Even the most loyal hearts can
only go unrequited for so long
before it moves on.

6-14-15 / j. iron word

THE CHASE

I miss you, but I will not chase
what does not want to be caught.

4-12-16 / j. iron word

BEST GOODBYE

Sometimes saying goodbye is
saying hello to someone new and
that very same goodbye is the
best thing you will ever do.

8-7-16 / j. iron word

SOMEONE NEW

One day I won't be there, one day
you won't be able to take me for
granted, one day I'll belong to
someone new.

12-2-15 / j. iron word

THE BROKEN PART

There is a part of love that people
warn us about but never listen to
until it's too late, the broken part.

12-10-15 / j. iron word

BROKEN SLEEP

There is nothing more painful
than falling asleep with a broken
heart.

1-3-16 / j. iron word

BLIND

I would have died for you, but
what you did killed me and that I
never saw coming.

3-13-16 / j. iron word

A WAY

Sometimes the hardest steps in love are the ones you take away from it.

12-3-15 / j. iron word

THE STORY

Behind every lost soul is a story of
a broken heart.

2-12-16 / j. iron word

VACANT LOVE

We come for love and stay for it,
even when it is not present
anymore.

12-10-15 / j. iron word

JUST LOVED

I know I have been broken, but I
don't need to be fixed, just loved.

9-29-15 / j. iron word

CAPABLE

While I am perfectly capable of
walking this planet without you,
it would be the loneliest journey
knowing you exist.

4-3-15 / j. iron word

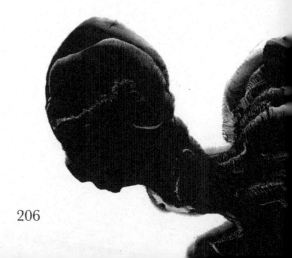

THE YOU

I miss the you I fell in love with,
the you that loved me back.

5-5-16 / j. iron word

UNDERSTANDING

He didn't have to say a
word and neither did
she. She was hurt and
that's all he needed to
feel.

Although it was not
him who caused the
pain, he couldn't help
but feel to blame for
not protecting her.

Reaching his arm
around her he pulled
her close and their
hearts beat as one.

She was not alone.

9-13-14 / j. iron word

Too Much

It was
the simple things
I needed that were
too much for you
to give that
ended our
story.

12-7-15 / j. iron word

PIECES

Maybe we will never
be more than friends,
or maybe just maybe
we will be lovers and
friends.

But for now I will love
you in pieces even though
all I want is your whole.

10-8-16 / j. iron word

CRIPPLED

Lies hurt, but
when they are from
the mouth of someone you loved,
they cripple your heart and
handicap your ability to love
again.

8-18-15 / j. iron word

THERE'S A DIFFERENCE

Not everyone's
"I love you," means the same
thing.

7-9-15 / j. iron word

ANYWAY

I wasn't supposed to
fall, but I did anyway.
It isn't supposed to
hurt, but it does
anyway. I will be okay,
because life goes on
anyway.

11-9-16 / j. iron word

213

LAST CHAPTER

IMMORTAL

How do you write
of a love that never
dies?

A love that could never
be described as perfect,
but whose darkness still
held an unconditional beauty.

A bond between a
king and a queen
who in the end wore
heather colored crowns.

A pair that learned
life was not always
living in between the
raindrops, but dancing
together in them.

A story of a love so pure,
even a slipping mind
could not touch.

An adoration that
did not stop merely
because her heart did.

An endearment
so strong he smiled
in the face of death,
because together
again they would
be.

How do you
write of a love
that never dies?

You tell their story.

    - j. iron word

THE COMPANY OF NONE

I peeked over the
shadows to see Earth,
but it was only once.

The warmth of the life
I witnessed and the colors
they came with opened
my eyes to distance
between myself and
the rest of humanity.

But alone I am not.
The dark side of the
moon is a cold and
lifeless place. It
however feels
as desolate as me.

Here, I am
accompanied by my
thoughts and in
the presence of none
I find I am never
misunderstood.

In the silence
I often question which
is louder, my thoughts
or my heartbeat.

Sometimes I want to run,
but how can you run from
yourself.

I try and try to smile and
laugh but fall short of
stopping to breathe.

Alone is not all I want to
know, but seems it is
what I know best.

-j. iron word

THE EXAMPLE

To be different is
to be ones true self
and there is no greater
bravery in a world of
mirrors.

My Hell on Earth was
the distance between who
the world thought I was
and who I actually was.

A disappointment
however, was never what I was.

I did what was asked
of me, before it was
ever spoken. I acted in
the manner in which,
I was expected to act.

I lived a life that made
others happy, asking
what they wanted
and needed.

I was the example
others pointed
to and I shined,
even though all
I wanted to do
was fade away
and be forgotten.

Inside lost is all I was,
spinning out of control
I realized I was the problem.
I never once asked what
I wanted, what I needed?

Unsteady I crumbled
and fell, breaking into
a million fragments. Even
my shards were nothing
more than a disappointment.
But I had finally achieved
perfection; I was the perfect
example of everything not to be.

- j. iron word

Begin Again

Staring into a blank
space, my mind is
in a frenzy, but I
focus.

While I know there
is nothing new to this,
it is all completely new.

I have been here before,
but I never thought I
would have to be here
again. Yet here I am,
beginning again.

All the planning in
the world could
not plan for the change
of direction in my life.

Change however
happened and with
it I have learned that
it is one of life's inevitable
truths.

A truth that at times is
a measure of growth and
other times as in now,
is an unforeseen
change in direction.

One that I can either
live with and allow it
to ultimately control
my destination or one
I can see as an opportunity
to take over my life's compass.

One thing is now clear
I am no longer staring into a
blank space as I am focused
on my life's tomorrow.

- j. iron word

FLAWED

I have never been
a thing of beauty.

Awkward has been
what I have always
known best, what
I am most comfortable
in.

A misunderstood
mental drifter I am
happiest in thought.

Even standing in a
sea of strangers, I am
miles away from
everyone.

Not that I do not
like people because
I do. Seeing their joy
and wonder I find
happiness in even
the most distant of them.

People praise me and
I thank them, but inside
I push away, because I
do not see what they do.

Alone again, I look in the
mirror at my scarred heart,
I can remember where I
earned every scar.

I smile, and for once it is
genuine; knowing that
flawed is the only real
beauty in the world.

- j. iron word

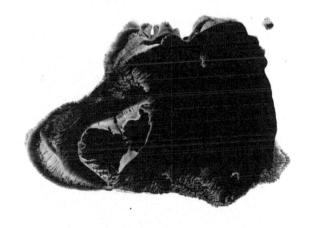

HOME

There are moments
in life when you have
to leap and there are
others when all it takes
is a step.

Placing one foot
in front of the other,
I step.

As I do I realize I
am not alone, but
accompanied by
one.

A one that feels like
home even on an
open road.

The road ahead
twists and bends,
but my one and I
push on.

Even with the air
full of uncertainty
I am somehow
certain, this is
my path, our path.

The stone pavement
beneath my feet, our
feet, is solid.

With my one's hand
in mine I know I am
no longer a one, but
a part of a two.

A two that is home
even while on an
open road.

- j. iron word

YOUR EYES

In your eyes is where
I met hope and said
goodbye to sorrow.

In your eyes is where
I know truth lives, despite
being surrounded by a
world of lies.

In your eyes
is where I see
everything I have
ever wanted to be,
but never thought
I could or would,
but now I know I am.

In your eyes is where
I find myself lost and
found all at once.

In your eyes is where
I forget the existence
of darkness and only
know the warmth of light.

In your eyes is where
I am loved unconditionally
even with my imperfections
in plain sight.

In your eyes is where
I see a future, that
makes me forget
my past.

In your eyes is where
where I know the joy
of finally being home
and where I wish to
say my last goodbye.

- j. iron word

RESILIENT CHAOS

She was a symbol
of peace, but her life
was not always so.

She had lived a life that
was not always easy,
one that taught her
the meaning of
resiliency.

It was in those moments
that were meant to break
her however, that she found
her greatest strength,
herself.

Although those days
were behind her, she still
could not help but remember
where she came from.

All the lessons she learned
had shaped her heart and
illuminated her soul.

Not everyone could be her,
but not everyone was meant
to be her, she was one of a kind.

- j. iron word

We Happened First

Life happens, but it wasn't
supposed to happen to us,
but it did anyway.

We however are different,
we are love, the type of
love that doesn't dim
or fade.

Life happened and almost
took you away, but you stayed
and through the pain and the
struggle you continued to love
me anyway.

We are different, we share a
connection that others dream
of. One that is stronger now
after life almost took us away.

Life happened, but we happened
first and that can never be taken
away.

- j. iron word

THE MIDDLE

Love is not always easy,
but it is love nonetheless.

We did not make
it to happily ever after, but
we loved.

We gave it our all,
loving each other even
during the times when
it was difficult to
love ourselves.

We built a life together,
with a family to call our
own.

In their eyes
I see you and me and
all the hopes and dreams
we had when we met.

We did not make it to
forever, but we loved
in the middle.

A middle that made
a person with hopes
and dreams of their
own.

j. iron word

A Name

What's in a name,
but a face with a
soul unlike any other.

What's in a name,
but an uncontrollable
smile or frown.

What's in a name,
but a hand to hold
with an arm and a
body to hug.

What's in a name,
but a reoccurring
dream.

What's in a name,
but a love for
someone that left
you forever changed.

What's in a name,
but a million memories
that can never be forgotten.

What's in a name,
but the skip of a beating
heart.

What's in a name,
but a time and place
when you said hello
or goodbye.

What's in a name,
but every single thing.

- j. iron word